# SNAPPED SHOESTRINGS

LITTLE

POEMS

ABOUT

REALLY

ANNOYING

STUFF.

**WRITTEN BY:**

Bill Bridgeman,
Dana David,
Cheryl Gaines,
Bill Gray,
Cheryl Hawkinson,
Jim Howard,
Allyson Jones,
Kevin Kinzer,
Mark Oatman,
Dan Taylor
and Myra Zirkle

# MAYBE YOU'D LIKE TO COUNT MY FILLINGS?

Sometimes I'm amazed
at the things people say,
Like "How old are you, really?"
and "How much do you weigh?"
"What did that cost?"
"Do you color your hair?"
"Is that your real nose?"
"What size do you wear?"
Questions like these
put me right in the mood
where I just want to ask
"Are you always so rude?"

# THE NOT-SO-ODD COUPLE

He likes the window open,
I like the window shut.
He orders pizza with sausage,
I would choose anything but.
He seizes the day in the city,
I'd rather be on a farm.
He's a fan of cold showers,
I like them pleasantly warm.
He adores classical music,
I prefer "Twist and Shout."
We have what it takes to be married—
Things to argue about.

# HE LAWN RANGER

Mow, mow, mow the lawn
in the afternoon,
Trim it, edge it, clip it, and
it grows back way too soon.

# THE DINER'S LAMENT

I have a real dilemma
for which I could use direction—
How to keep the smoke from drifting
into the "No Smoking" section.

# SUCH A DEAL

I ordered a salad,
they brought me the soup,
And under the table
was some kind of goop.
The water was warm
and the french fries were cold,
The waiter was new
but the breadsticks were old.
The chance I'll come back
isn't more than a vapor,
Unless there's a coupon
again in the paper.

# BLANK BOX

I sit, I stare,

I curse my fate,

I fidget and I pout,

I rant, I rave,

I kick the set,

and still the cable's out.

**12:00...**
**12:00...**
**12:00...**

Here's a quick and easy way
to set your VCR:
Just set it in your driveway
and hit it with your car.

# STILL HOLDING

There's one thing that I've figured out,
though I'm not terribly clever—
When some people say
"I'll put you on hold,"
they mean "Good-bye forever."

# NOTE TO TELESALES PEOPLE

Call me a miser,

call me a crank,

call me a grouchy old sinner—

Call me a whiner,

call me a grump,

just don't call me during my dinner!

# FASHION
# QUESTION

Why do the world's
fashion designers
think we all have
tiny be-hinders?

# SMILES

You smile at him,
he smiles back.
Things are going swell.
He could be the one, you know,
you just can never tell.
But as his smile becomes a laugh,
you start to sink in grief—
Perhaps what he's been smiling at
is the chocolate on your teeth.

# MOVIE CRITIC'S CORNER

I knew, somehow, that you would find me
and, of course, you'd sit behind me—
Movies wouldn't be complete
without some yakking parakeet
like you to talk me off my seat.
I love a Stupid Comment-fest!
And after all, you must have guessed,
I didn't come to see the show—
I came to hear how much you know!

# NOT ENOUGH FOR YOU?

Here's hoping there's a spot reserved
in that place that's warm as can be
For drivers who zip into spaces
just ahead of me!

# A TRUE TEST

There's one way to tell
if the water's hot—
Is it my turn to shower?
Then probably not.

# METEOR-OLOGY

Predicting the weather
is easy to do,
If you want it to snow,
just wear your new shoes,
If you want a hot day
have the driveway retarred,
If you want it to rain—
wash the car.

# HURRY UP AND WAIT

I make a quick trip to the bank,
I only have a minute.
The line I choose moves right along,
that is, until I'm in it!

# MYSTERY MUG

Of all the misnomers
that I've ever heard,
"coffee machine"
is perhaps most absurd.
The liquid dispensed
may be brownish and hot,
But one thing is certain—
coffee, it's not.

# CUT!

My husband's the family director,
our movies are always unique.
With an eye to the lens he yells "Action!"
securing the shot that he seeks.
He titles each film that he edits,
he's truly a mini-cam nut.
Now if there were just some way to get him
to stop zooming in on my butt.

# TIME MARCHES ON

I got my hair perfect,
the cowlick stayed down.
The waves waved, the curls curled,
it was good all around.
I got my hair perfect,
I treasured this day,
Till I checked one more mirror
and saw my first gray.

# FATAL ERROR

I used to have a typewriter
with a key that stuck a little—
Sometimes the ribbon would unwind
and I'd have to reach in and fiddle.
So I put it away in the trunk of my car
with an unexplained feeling of dread,
Took it downtown on a Monday
and got a computer instead.
I sat down and wrote a long letter—
my language could not have been fairer...

I pecked at the key that would print it,
but the screen only said "Fatal Error!"
I sat as I stared and I wondered
at the faux pas I must have committed,
Then I thought of my trusty typewriter
and wondered out loud why I did it.
"Fatal Error," the blinking screen taunted,
and I was the one who had made it.
My typewriter may have been sloppy,
but it never typed something...then ate it.

# NOT A CHEF YET

Cajun cooking,
I haven't learnt—
When I blacken something,
it just tastes burnt.

# PILLOW TALK

I slap at the middle,
I beat from both ends,
I fold it, unfold it,
and fold it again.
I fluff it, smooth it,
get so mad I could throw it!
There's a comfortable spot
in this pillow,
I know it!

# SNOOZE
## PAPER

I think an open newspaper
is something to be read,
Of course, my cat knows better—
it's actually a bed.

# THE PERFECT ARGUMENT

There's one thing wrong
With owning a gerbil—
They smell ter-bil!

# HOMEOWNER'S LAMENT

The handyman
for whom I would kill
Is the one who shows up
when he says he will.

# NOT-SO-CLEAN SWEEP

I despise it when my domesticity
is snagged by fate or static electricity—
Hand-feeding my sweeper some piece of fluff,
I think, "This sucks, but not enough!"

# PICNIC

White shorts and mustard,
skin turned red by sun,
Ants, flies and bumblebees—
where's the part that's fun?

# SWEET SURRENDER

When all the world seems against me,
and I'm feeling crushed and beat,
 I hold this cherished knowledge—
mosquitos think I'm sweet.

# REMEMBER ME?

We bumped into each other
while standing in a line,
She said, "So glad to see ya!"
and "Yes, I'm doing fine."
We talked about the kids,
our lawns and all our pets,
Their inoculations,
good weeders and our vets.
The chat was so delightful,
but it was such a shame,
I didn't have the slightest clue—
now, just what was her name?

# WHOOPS!

I said, "Congratulations!"
"The dad must be so proud!"
About the thrills of parenting,
I went on long and loud.
I said she seemed to glow with joy
there's no mistake detecting,
She thanked me, then replied,
"That's nice, but I'm not expecting."

# THE RUNNER, HE STUMBLES

The runner, he stumbles from bed
as the hills receive the sun's kisses,
He tiptoes across the bedroom
so as not to awaken the Mrs.,
He pulls on his old running pants
and his Boston Marathon shirt,
He places a bandage on his middle toe
so yesterday's blister won't hurt.

He zips on a faded old jacket
and pulls on some blue cotton gloves,
He tugs a sweatband over his head—
yes, this is the time that he loves.
He's just about ready to run now,
as he pulls on his old tattered cap,
Then tightens the lace on his sneakers
and feels the shoestring go SNAP!

# WRAPPED
## WITH LOVE

I took my time
in selecting the bow,
Made each crease straight
and taped it just so.
My corners were neat—
the gift looked so nice!
Now if only I'd remembered
to remove the price.

# FASHION SENSE

I've got so many sweaters,
I can't tell one from another.
But you'll never see me wear them
'cause I got them from my mother.

# CHEF'S SURPRISE

You invent a new casserole—
it's really the best,
It tastes quite divine—
except when there's guests.

# FIRST IMPRESSIONS

I made an outstanding impression
at a dinner party last night—
My banter was witty and charming,
and I was extremely polite.
My insightful remarks were well-taken,
I was truly a wonderful guy,
The whole evening would have been perfect—
if only I'd zipped up my fly.

# KICK ME WITH NEW SHOES

I bought some new shoes
'cause they were so nice,
Then the next day,
they went to half price.

# WHAT'S THAT STENCH?

There's nothing like a giant whiff
of bad perfume, especially if
it's with you on an elevator.
(Ms. Stinko exits. See ya later!)
And now the folks from other floors
get on and choke—and think it's yours!

# FINDERS, KEEPERS

A diet is always a pain in the butt,
still, I don't think I'd really mind it
If every time I lost some weight
I didn't look in the mirror and find it.

# AT THE GYM

If looks could kill,
I'd cast a glance
toward the inventor
of spandex pants.

# SUMMER

No place on earth is hotter
than the dashboard of a car,
Which is why it makes me sad to know
that's where my CDs are.

# CHANGE

I'd wash off the bugs that are stuck in the grille
and the muck and the mud from a drive up a hill.
I'd wax that old paint till it shined just like new,
I'd clean off the floor mats and dust the dash, too.
This car would be spotless, I'd get such a thrill
if only the changer would take my darn bill.

# RELATIVITY

How can an hour last so long
between 4 p.m. and 5?
And yet a week can go so fast
when vacation time arrives.

# CARRY ON

I packed a sweater for cool nights
and shorts in case it's sunny,
Some jeans, some sandals, gym shoes,
and a T-shirt that is funny.
A suit if dinner's formal
and another suit for swimming,
One shirt with dots and one with plaid
and stripes (you know, they're slimming!).
My bags are jammed with worthwhile stuff,
they really are quite full,
Which makes it truly tragic
that they're bound for Istanbul.

# WINDSHIELD
# WIPERS

You turn them on,
you turn them off—
There isn't any rain,
just drizzly stuff.
It's not wet enough
to wipe it clear—
It's just enough
to leave a smear.

# GETTING NOWHERE FAST

See that guy in the car ahead
as he darts from lane to lane?
Left, then right, then left, then right,
then to the left again?
What exactly does he gain
from his erratic flight?
The chance to spend more time than I
waiting at the light!

# BABY PICTURES

I think I've discovered the reason
for each baby picture I've seen,
The parents just want proof that sometimes
the baby is quiet and clean.

# EAR PLUGS, PLEASE

"Mary Had a Little Lamb"
is not my favorite tune,
Especially since
my kid just learned
To play it on the bassoon.

# THANKS FOR THE ADVICE

"Have a good day!"
said the cheery voice.
Does she think I'd have
a bad one by choice?

# BURGERS AND WHAT?!

The drive-through sure is handy,
you can get your food real quick.
It's warm, it's cheap, it's tasty—
yeah, those guys don't miss a trick.
You get it home and settle down,
it's fast-food-supper night!
You open up the bags and find
they didn't get it right.

# DEAR PUBLISHER

I'd like to read
from front to back
your illustrious magazine,
So would you please
eliminate
the inserts in between?

# TABLOID HELL

When I'm in the checkout line,
I don't want to read about Elvis.
I don't want to see some silicone blonde
with no hips, no tummy, no pelvis.
I don't care if a poltergeist killed J.F.K.
or if angels wear jeans from the Gap.
I don't care if Bigfoot's a psychic—
tell him to shut his primitive yap.
I don't care if Roseanne's abduction by aliens
caused her to go on a diet,
And if the world is, indeed, at an end,
Just gimme some peace and quiet
instead of this screaming tabloid hell—
Oh, who am I kidding. I'll buy it!

# BAD TASTE

A small dilemma, certainly,
but one that causes grief—
Trying to drink your orange juice
once you've brushed your teeth.

# OOPS!
## SORRY, MOM!

There's one magnetic attraction
that scientists ought to explore—
It's whatever draws wet, muddy feet
to a just-mopped floor!

# ARGUMENT FOR CALL-WAITING

I call a friend,

but the line is busy—

So I pour a soda,

nice and fizzy.

I try again,

but the line is still tied—

How could it be

that she's still occupied?

One more time

I try the phone—

Only to find

now there's nobody home.

# CAT HAIR

Everywhere,
cat hair.
On the stair,
in the chair,
in the air—
everywhere.
The oddest thing to me is that
there's still a lot left on the cat.

# BROWN BAG
## BLUES

Liquid yogurt,
stale bread,
Is tuna really gray?
Bendy pickles,
shattered chips—
I brought my lunch today.

# THIS IS CRISP?

They call it a crisper drawer.

Am I a simp,

or is it designed

to make vegetables limp?

# DULLSVILLE

If you shave your beard
and in its place
you're left with toilet paper face,
here's a thought that just might soothe—
someone's legs are really smooth.

# WAISTED
## EFFORT

When you try to
dress more youthful,
it's your gut that
keeps you truthful.

# SLUDGE

I dunked a whole donut
in my coffee cup,
But to my surprise,
only half came back up.

# HAPPENS EVERY TIME

The one day that you're late for work,
you can bet your very last dime,
Is the day the boss gathers everyone
for a meeting on "being on time."

# MAN'S BEST
## WHAT?

When it starts to snow,

the dog has to go.

# LIBRARY LAMENT

No matter what
the book's about,
If I need it—
it's checked out.

# A CLEANSING PRAYER

I have my own religion,
though some might find it odd—
Sacrificing stockings
to the washer-dryer god.

# WHY BOTHER?

I clip 'em,

I sort 'em,

I file 'em

and then,

I leave

the *@#%

coupons

at home

once again.

# SKINNY CLOTHES

You pull, you push,
you stretch and bend,
But those jeans
won't fit again.

# PICTURE IMPERFECT

I don't know whether
to cry or laugh—
I just saw me
in a photograph!

# SCRATCH OR DIE

Is there anything quite

like an insect bite

in a place you can't publicly scratch?

It's especially fun

if there's not just one

but a whole big bug-bitten batch.

So you cross your legs

as that itch just begs

to be scratched, though scratching be brief—

Till at last you're alone

and you scratch and you groan

and you fall over dead from relief.

# SEEING STARS

After endless hours of standing in line,
I've got concert tickets - I'm feeling fine!
But from where I sit, my only hope
will be borrowing a telescope.

# A BRIEF MESSAGE TO PEOPLE WITH CAR PHONES

All I'm trying to do
is get back home,
So make a choice, Pal—
drive or use the phone!

# TO MARKET, TO MARKET

Congratulations, Coupon Queen,
ahead of me in line—
You just saved 37 cents
and wasted all my time.

# THE PRODIGY

I can't refold a road map,
I have an aversion to it.
What makes me even madder is,
my 3-year-old can do it.

# A THUMP AS YOU DRIVE OFF

Two different shades of lipstick
are there to fit my mood,
Some tissues and a nail file,
a coupon for junk food,
Childhood pictures and a license,
half a chocolate bar,
A comb, a brush and mirror,
hand cream in a jar—
A purse is full of things you need,
no matter where you are,
Unless you do what I did—
and leave it on top of the car.

# MY **PAL** JOE

I want a cup of coffee.

Is that so much to want?

Just a good ol' cup of joe—

if you want me to be blunt.

Do I want cappuccino?

Gracious me, no!

Do I want latte?

Certainly notte!

Half caf?

You make me laugh!

Java! Jamocha! A mug of mud!

That's the thing I'm craving, Bud!

Keep your cups of scalded cream.

As for me—just bring caffeine.

That's all I need

to make it through...

OK...perhaps a donut, too.

# MERGE OR PURGE

The concept of an entrance ramp,
O Stupid Fellow Driver,
Is no great mystery—to solve it
doesn't take MacGyver.
There is one single, simple rule
for merging with the flow,
That rule consists of three short words—
Go, Go, and Go.
But you have stopped, so now
look back, you've got an entourage!
Their hand signals suggest, next time,
just stay in your garage!

# TURN, TURN, TURN

There's this thing about driving
some lunkheads should learn—
When you turn on your turn signal,
TURN!

# SNOW JOB

First you set your VCR
to record your favorite show,
Then you rewind,
only to find
Two hours of hissing snow.

# WAITER, I'D LIKE ANOTHER SHIRT, PLEASE

The restaurant's expensive,
the ambience, just right,
The silver gleams discreetly
in the glow of candlelight,
But it's hard to be a sophisticate
(I may as well be blunt),
When you've spilled a blob of grey poupon
directly down your front.

# BREAKFAST OF ALSO-RANS

It's morning,
so off to the cupboard I go,
Expecting to find
a nice big bowl of "O's,"
Instead, what I find
to my utter disgust...
Cereal dust.

# RONIC, ISN'T IT?

Low-fat cookies, low-fat shakes,
and low-fat brownies
for goodness' sake!
There's a low-fat version
of this and that
as far as you can see—
They make a low-fat everything,
but still no low-fat me.

# GOLDEN WHAT?

It's not a cause for revelry
or joyous celebration—
The day the music of your youth
makes the oldies station.

# THE TENNIS INJURY

I have a tennis injury—
my foot is in a cast,
I show it like a badge of pride
to everyone I pass.
"Trying to return a serve?"
"That's right!" I answer, "You bet!"
And hope that no one ever finds out
that I broke it when jumping the net.

# RECIPE FOR A HEADACHE

I open a high kitchen cabinet

And find that the cupboard is bare—

So I squat down and open

another one, hopin'

The thing I'm lookin' for's there.

But I just can't find

whatever it is—

Though the second cabinet's full.

I stand, and the door

that I opened before

Has no trouble finding my skull.

# INVOLUNTARY DIETING

Should I eat the last of the ice cream?
My inner voice tells me "Just do it!"
 I open the freezer, my face falls a mile—
when I find someone else beat me to it!